VAUX HA
FREE PUB

D0098300

APACHE HELICOPTER: THE AH-64

VAUX HALL BRANCH
FREE PUBLIC LIBRARY

Matthew Pitt

HIGH interest books

Children's Press
High Interest Books
A Division of Grolier Publishing
New York / London / Hong Kong / Sydney
Danbury, Connecticut

Photo Credits: Cover, p. 19, 22, 24, 30, 32, 39, 43 © Photri; p. 5, 36 © John H. Clark/Corbis; p. 6 © David Lee/Corbis; p. 9 © Hulton-Deutsch Collection/Corbis; p. 10, 12, 16, 20, 41 © George Hall/Corbis; p. 15, 29 © Corbis; p. 26 © Bettmann/Corbis; p. 35 © af/mil/photos.
Contributing Editors: Robert Kirkpatrick and Mark Beyer
Book Design: Michael DeLisio

Visit Children's Press on the Internet at:
http://publishing.grolier.com

Library of Congress Cataloging-in-Publication Data

Pitt, Matthew.
  Apache helicopter : the AH-64 / by Matthew Pitt.
    p. cm. – (High-tech military weapons)
  Includes bibliographical references and index.
  Summary: Provides general information about helicopters and specific
    facts about the features and operation of the Apache helicopter.
  ISBN 0-516-23336-X (lib. bdg.) – ISBN 0-516-23536-2 (pbk.)
  1. Apache (Attack helicopter) – Juvenile literature. 2. United States.
  Army—Aviation—Juvenile literature. [1. Apache (Attack helicopter) 2.
    Helicopters.] I.
  Title. II. Series.

UG1233.P57 2000
623.7'46047—dc21   00-024369

Copyright © 2000 by Rosen Book Works, Inc.
All rights reserved. Published simultaneously in Canada.
Printed in the United States of America.
1 2 3 4 5 6 7 8 9 10 R 05 04 03 02 01 00

CONTENTS

INTRODUCTION

You are standing in a field. The sky is bright and free of clouds. Suddenly, you hear a low, whirring noise. It gets louder by the second. Out of the corner of your eye, you see a dark blip in the sky. As the object gets closer, the grass stirs. The trees begin to whip around, creating the sound of waves crashing on a beach. You hear the sound of motors. You see large blades spinning wildly. Wind whips against your face. The ground feels shaky as the machine touches down.

Is this a UFO? You look closer at this air monster. Armor and missile launchers gleam in the sunlight. There is a pilot in the cockpit. The pilot is human, not alien! You're not looking at a spaceship. You are face-to-face with the AH-64A Apache helicopter.

The Apache was an exciting new addition to U.S. military aircraft. In this book, you will get to read all about the AH-64A. So turn the page and prepare to be blown away!

Close-up view of a killing machine: the AH-64 Apache.

CHAPTER 1

THE HISTORY OF HELICOPTERS

For centuries, great thinkers have tried to design helicopters. In ancient times, the Chinese created a toy that could lift in the air when a child spun it. In the sixteenth century, Leonardo da Vinci drew sketches of an invention that looked much like a helicopter. However, the engines needed to power da Vinci's machine would not be invented for nearly four hundred years.

The first helicopters appeared in the beginning of the twentieth century. They had rotors turned by engines. Early helicopter

Leonardo da Vinci sketched a helicopterlike device. This model was based on da Vinci's drawings.

inventors had trouble perfecting the rotor system. Helicopters would lift off the ground and then spin out of control or flip over.

Then, in 1907, French inventor Paul Cornu came up with the idea of having two rotors on a helicopter. The main rotor would create lift. The second rotor, on the back of the helicopter, would help to balance the aircraft. To prove that his idea would work, Cornu built a two-rotor helicopter. During a test flight, he kept it in flight for twenty seconds. This was not a long time, but it proved that helicopters could work. As technology became more advanced in the twentieth century, helicopters became better. They could stay in the air longer.

HOW HELICOPTERS FLY

The main difference between an airplane and a helicopter is the direction in which it takes off. An airplane must go forward as it

The first helicopters were used to deliver mail.

takes off. It runs along the ground until it has enough energy to lift into the sky. A helicopter lifts off vertically (straight up). A helicopter also can hover (fly in place). Whether a helicopter is lifting up or landing, it doesn't need any runway at all. Helicopters can lift off or land in places a plane cannot, such as in a jungle clearing or on a building top.

BLADE RUNNERS

How can helicopters lift off and hover? The secret is in the rotors (spinning blades) on

Don't get too close! The Apache AH-64 has some powerful blades.

top of a helicopter. Motors power the rotors and make them spin faster and faster. When these rotors begin spinning, they push down air. The air hits the ground and then bounces back. This air pushes the helicopter upward. This process is called lift. Gravity tries to keep the helicopter from lifting. To stay in the air, a helicopter's rotors must create enough lift to overcome gravity.

Rotors do not just create lift. They also steer the helicopter. When the pilot turns the helicopter, he does so by tilting the rotors. The 'copter goes in the direction in which the rotors are tilted.

SEED OF AN IDEA

To understand how a helicopter works, you can begin by looking in nature. You'll notice maple seeds seem to have wings that look just like helicopter blades. Have you ever seen a maple seed fall to the ground? It doesn't fall straight down. Instead, the seed flutters gently to the ground, spinning and spinning around. The wing of the seed catches air and keeps it afloat. Now imagine that the seed can spin very fast. It would stay in the air. The design of helicopter rotors are based on this idea.

The Bell 209 Cobra "Snake" was one of the first
helicopters to have missile launchers.

'COPTERS IN THE MILITARY

In World War I (1914–1918), an early form of
the helicopter was used for some military
missions. However, the first widespread use
of helicopters in combat did not come until
the Vietnam War (1967–1973). The U.S. military liked how helicopter pilots could fly
through jungles and land in small clearings

to pick up wounded troops. Some helicopters, such as the Bell 209 Cobra "Snake"
and the Gyrodyne QH-50, had missile
launchers on their sides. The QH-50 even
used special cameras to help pilots see at
night. These cameras read the heat that
machines and people give off. This type of
camera is called an infrared camera.

BUILDING A BETTER HELICOPTER

In the early 1970s, the U.S. Army decided to
put money into making a new helicopter. The
Army wanted to make sure that the next time
the United States went to war, it would have
faster and more powerful helicopters. At that
time, U.S. officials were concerned that the
United States might someday be involved in
a conflict with the Soviet Union. The Army
knew that the Soviet military had many more
attack helicopters than did the United States.
The Soviets also had powerful tanks. If the

United States had to go to war against the Soviet Union, it would need helicopters that could fight enemy helicopters and attack enemy tanks.

In 1973, U.S. Army officials asked a number of companies to design a new helicopter. The Army looked at all the designs to find the one that would be the fastest, strongest, and most durable. The Army felt the design made by the Hughes company (later called McDonnell Douglas) was the best. The Army asked this company to make a model of the exciting new aircraft.

FAST FACT

The first helicopters were powered by bicycle wheels. The pilot pedaled the wheels. The wheels were hooked up to the rotors. When the pilot pedaled, he or she made the rotors spin.

The YAH-64 was an early prototype of the Apache.

Taking Flight

Hughes spent the next two years building a prototype (early model) of its helicopter. The prototype, called the YAH-64, made its first flight in 1975. What looked good as a drawing looked great flying in the sky! The following year, the U.S. military gave McDonnell Douglas a multimillion-dollar contract to build more of this impressive aircraft. In 1982, the helicopter was named the Apache AH-64A.

CHAPTER 2

THE APACHE AND ITS CREW

In 1984, the Army began to train pilots to fly the Apache AH-64A. These lucky pilots must have felt like kids let loose at a candy store! The new helicopter came loaded with features never before seen on a helicopter.

ARMED TO THE TEETH

The main use of the Apache helicopter is as an attack aircraft. The Apache is loaded with all kinds of the latest and most powerful weapons. When it comes to weaponry, no other helicopter can compare to the Apache.

The Apache is flown by a two-person crew.

In fact, military experts have said that the Apache is less like a helicopter, and more like a tank with wings.

HELLFIRE IN THE SKY

Apaches are armed with sixteen missiles. These missiles have the code name Hellfire. The Hellfire missiles are the Apache's strongest weapons. They can punch through the toughest armor made. Apaches also carry up to seventy-six rockets. These rockets are fired from the sides of the helicopter. The places from which the rockets are fired are called pods. Rockets are used against ground troops, supply trucks and trains, and buildings. Finally, the Apache has a 30mm automatic cannon underneath its fuselage (center section). This cannon can fire more than a thousand rounds of high-powered bullets in just a few minutes!

One Apache AH-64 can carry all these firearms.

THICK SKIN

The body of the Apache is made of the strongest metals on Earth. It is built with the protective armor of a tank. It can withstand hits from most guns and small explosives. The Apache is also very durable. Through tests and battles, the military has found that pilots can keep an Apache helicopter in the air for more than half an hour after it has taken a direct hit.

This crew is ready for action!

CREW OF TWO

Two crew members operate an Apache. The copilot/gunner sits in front, near the nose of the helicopter. From this position, he has a clear view of all targets. The head pilot sits above and behind the copilot. The place where the crew sits is called the cockpit. The cockpit is protected by armor plates and very thick plastic shields. Its armor protects the crew from bullets and small explosives. If an object were to break through the Apache cockpit, the crew is still well protected. Both crew members are strapped into special seats. These seats are made of a material called Kevlar. Kevlar is the same material that is used to make bulletproof vests.

Crash-Proof

The Apache is one mean fighting machine. It is very hard to bring down. However, if an Apache is disabled, it is well equipped for a crash landing. The Apache's wheels, rotors, and tail are built so that they crush neatly on impact during a crash. This may sound dangerous, but actually it is a safety measure. If these parts collapse away from the cockpit during a crash, the crew is less likely to be struck by broken wreckage.

LOCKING IN

The AH-64A carries a special computer system onboard. This system is called the target acquisition designation sight (TADS). The TADS computer points an intense (strongly focused) beam of light on the target. This intense light beam is called a laser. When the pilot launches the helicopter's Hellfire weapons, the missiles follow the laser beam.

The Apache AH-64 has special technology that allows pilots to fly it at night.

The TADS laser system is a near-perfect guide. It leads to a direct hit almost every time.

NIGHT FLIGHT

Until the Apache, most helicopters flew only during the day. Helicopter pilots could not see at night. The Apache came with special helmets that allow pilots to see at night. These helmets are called pilot night vision sensors (PNVS). The Apache has computer sensors that can detect things at night. When the pilots strap these helmets on, they see things with the help of these sensors. What would look like a dark night to you or me looks like a clear day to the Apache pilots. These helmets also allow the pilots to see further away, and to see more from side to side. Enemy pilots that try to sneak up on the Apache don't stand much of a chance!

SPEEDY SPINNERS

The Apache also is fast. Considering the number of missiles and rockets the Apache carries, its system of powerful rotors allow it to reach amazing flying speeds. The Apache can cruise at 150 miles (241.5 km) per hour for several hours straight. If it needs to, it can reach a top speed of 230 miles (370 km) per hour.

FAST FACT

You can buy computer games that let you "fly" an Apache helicopter.

CHAPTER 3

THE APACHE IN ACTION

From the time McDonnell Douglas delivered its new Apache AH-64As in 1984, it took five more years before they were used in combat. As soon as the U.S. military used its new Apaches, it found out it had an exciting new weapon.

PANAMA

The U.S. military first used the Apache in battle during the 1989 invasion of Panama. President George Bush wanted to capture and arrest General Manuel Noriega, the Panamanian leader, for actions against the

The Apache AH-64 was used in the invasion of Panama in 1989.

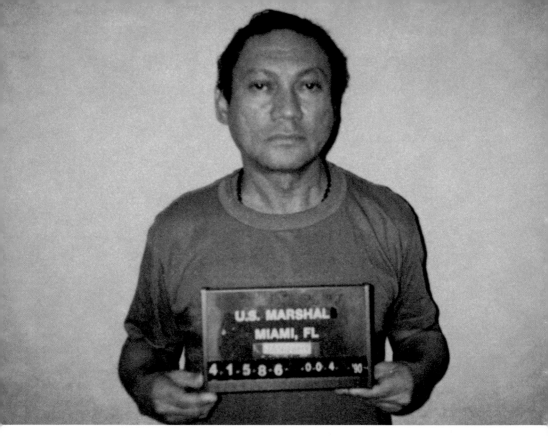

Apache units helped the U.S. military arrest
Panamanian leader General Manuel Noriega in 1989.

United States. This invasion was called
Operation Restore Hope. The Apache's PNVS
system was very helpful in launching night
attacks against the Panamanian military.
Thanks in part to Apache missions, the U.S.
military was able to overpower Panama's
forces. Noriega was arrested and brought to
the United States in 1990.

OPERATION DESERT STORM

The Apache was given its best chance to shine in 1991. This was the year of Operation Desert Storm, also known as the Gulf War. The Iraqi military, led by Saddam Hussein, had invaded the neighboring country of Kuwait. The United States decided to send forces overseas to free Kuwait.

Radar Wreckers

When U.S. forces attack enemy forces, they want to surprise the enemy. The military uses special computer systems to spot enemy forces from far away. These systems send out radio waves. If a plane is approaching, the radio waves bounce off the plane and go back to the computer. Then, the computer shows where the plane is. This system is called radar (RAdio Detecting And Ranging system).

In one of the first attacks of Desert Storm, eight Apaches destroyed two radar towers in western Iraq. Once the towers were destroyed, American jets could fly into Iraq without being spotted on radar. The Apaches finished this mission in only five minutes. This mission was proof that the new helicopter could do a job well and get the pilots out of harm's way quickly.

Sand Screens

Later in the Gulf War, quick-thinking Apache pilots turned the desert environment in Kuwait to their advantage. There are no hills or jungles or mountains—only sand. So the pilots flew very slowly and low to the ground. The low-flying helicopters kicked up lots of sand. The sand spun up into the rotors and then shot back out. The Apaches looked like sandstorms moving across the desert. Apache pilots used the sand as a screen. This helped them to sneak up on Iraqi forces. By the time a cease-fire was declared, 275

Apache helicopters were used to destroy these
Iraqi tanks during the Gulf War.

Apaches had destroyed more than five hundred tanks!

THE WORLD-FAMOUS APACHE

Since then, the Apache has done all that anyone could ask, and more. It has played a major role in helping U.S. forces to keep the peace in places such as Bosnia and Korea. The Apache was so successful that other countries wanted to have these helicopters

as well. McDonnell Douglas has sold more than one hundred Apache AH-64As to allies (friendly nations) of the United States, including Egypt, Great Britain, Greece, Israel, and Saudi Arabia. Clearly, everyone can see how impressive these attack helicopters are.

FAST FACT

In its first year with the Apache Longbow contract, personnel from the Army and Boeing trained more than 250 pilots to fly the new aircraft. The Royal Netherlands Air Force was the first foreign unit to complete the U.S. Army's Apache training course.

U.S. forces used the Apache to help end conflicts in Bosnia and Korea.

CHAPTER 4

NEW AND IMPROVED

The AH-64As were so effective in military operations that one would think these helicopters would be around forever. But in 1996, the Army decided to stop using this model of attack aircraft. Why? The helicopters had not performed poorly. Just the opposite: They had performed well for a very long time. The Army uses most aircraft for a little more than 1,000 hours. The fleet of AH-64As had flown for a total of 1 million hours! No matter how good these Apache aircraft were, eventually they would break down.

The improved Apache AH-64D.

Also, the Army realized that other countries were inventing better technology. The older the Apache AH-64A design got, the less effective it would be against new aircraft and new weapons. The Army still wanted to have an aircraft like the Apache, but it wanted to make it even better.

INTRODUCING THE LONGBOW

On February 11, 1996, the last four AH-64As were delivered to an Army squadron stationed in Korea. It was time to unveil a new machine. Just when people thought military helicopters couldn't get any better, they did. The Army introduced the new Apache model. It was the AH-64D, also known as the Apache Longbow.

A PROMISE KEPT

McDonnell Douglas had promised the Army a new Apache model that would be even

The newest generation of the
Apache is the AH-64D Longbow.

better than the old one. The AH-64D would
have new and exciting features. McDonnell
Douglas made six prototypes of the new
Longbow.

In 1995, the Army wanted to see just how
good this new aircraft was. It pitted the
Longbow prototypes against the original
Apache models in a practice air battle. The
pilots and gunners pretended that it was a
real fight, but they would not fire real missiles
or rockets. This type of fake battle is called a
combat simulation.

The Apache is a fierce, flying machine!

The exact results of this simulation are classified (kept secret), but we know one thing: The Apache Longbow beat the AH-64A! The AH-64D was quicker than the AH-64A and could make sharper turns. The Longbow's Hellfire missiles were better, too. They were more accurate and could hit targets that were farther away.

FORGETTABLE FIRE

The Longbow's missile shooters have a new feature called "fire and forget." Fire and forget is a special cooling system. As soon as the Longbow fires its Hellfire missiles, it quickly cools its own missile pods. Why is that important? Missiles from most enemy aircraft are heat seeking. When heat-seeking missiles are shot at aircraft, they go toward heat sources. If an AH-64A gave off a lot of heat from its missile pods, heat-seeking missiles would lock on the helicopter's pods and make a direct hit. Also, an AH-64A with hot missile pods would show up on infrared scanners. With its new cooling system, the Longbow is very hard to detect, especially at night or in bad weather. The fire-and-forget system may save the lives of Longbow pilots in the future!

A SMART SHOOTER

The Apache Longbow is the first helicopter

"smart" enough to know which enemy is most dangerous. The Longbow's computer system has memory banks in which it stores information about 128 different kinds of enemy military targets. The system also has an advanced radar detector. If the computer spots more than one enemy target, it goes through its memory to identify which type of aircraft or weapons are approaching. The computer lists the enemy targets in order based on which are the most dangerous. The target that is most likely to hurt the Longbow is the target at which the Longbow will fire. At the same time, the Longbow computer "talks" to other aircraft in the area. The Longbow's computer sends out signals to computers on other U.S. planes and helicopters. The signals tell all U.S. aircraft pilots what kind of enemy craft will be waiting for them. The Longbow does all of this in less than thirty seconds!

The Apache Longbow can stay in the air for
twenty-two out of twenty-four hours.

LONE GUNNER

The Longbow doesn't need as many repairs
between flights as did the AH-64A. The Army
can send the Longbow out on many missions
in a row without worrying that it will break
down. If needed, an Apache Longbow can fly
for twenty-two hours in a twenty-four-hour
day. It would need time only to refuel, load
new missiles, and let the tired pilot and gun-
ner out for a rest!

TOMORROW THE WORLD

The Apache Longbow did more than impress the Army. It impressed the world. A large aircraft company named Boeing bought McDonnell Douglas in 1997. Boeing continues to make the Apache Longbows for the U.S. Army. Also, Boeing recently sold Longbows to U.S. allies such as the Netherlands and Great Britain.

Fourteen Fatalities

The Apache Longbow is not flawless. In 1999, an AH-64D crashed in Albania during a nighttime test-flight. The plane burned up after the crash and both crew members died. This tragedy proved that no aircraft is perfectly safe. In fact, since the Apache first appeared in the U.S. military, fourteen pilots have died. After the million-plus hours of Apache missions, though, the Army considers this to be a low number.

The military is proud of the AH-64D.

UP, UP, AND AWAY

The Army is very pleased with the Apache Longbow. It can survive more direct hits than the AH-64A could, and the new Hellfire missiles are much more accurate than the older rockets. The Army is confident that the Apache Longbow will be their "top gun" for years to come!

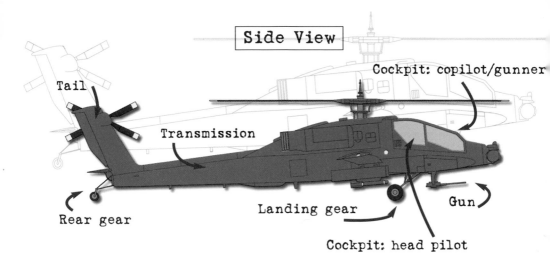

Side View

Tail

Cockpit: copilot/gunner

Transmission

Rear gear

Landing gear

Gun

Cockpit: head pilot

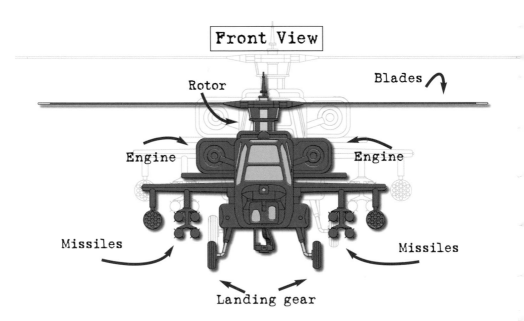

Front View

Rotor

Blades

Engine

Engine

Missiles

Missiles

Landing gear

AH-64 firing missiles to targets in war zones were very accurate and reliable.

Top View

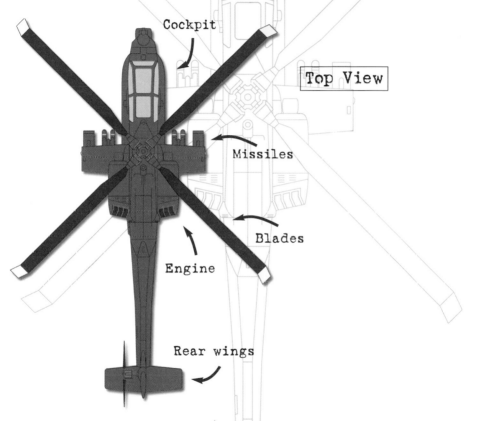

Cockpit

Missiles

Blades

Engine

Rear wings

	AH-64A Apache	AH-64D Apache Longbow
Length:	58 feet (17.7 m)	58.17 feet (17.73 m)
Height:	15.2 feet (4.64 m)	16.25 feet (4.95 m)
Wing span:	17 feet (5.2 m)	17.15 feet (5.227 m)

allies friendly nations

classified kept secret

cockpit the place where the crew sits

combat simulation battle practice

designation a title or class

fuselage the center of an aircraft where the crew and cargo are held

hover fly in place

lift a force of nature causing the helicopter to rise

liftoff the moment when a helicopter first takes flight

principle a rule about some natural force (such as gravity)

prototype an early model of a ship or aircraft

rotors spinning blades on top of a helicopter

vertically straight up

Hawkes, Nigel. *Planes and Other Flying Machines.* Brookfield, CT: Copper Beech Books, 1999.

Jennings, Terry. *Planes, Gliders, Helicopters, & Other Flying Machines.* New York: Larousse Kingfisher Chambers, Incorporated, 1993.

Kerrod, Robin. *Amazing Flying Machines.* New York: Alfred A. Knopf Books for Young Readers, 1992.

Schleifer, Jay. *Combat Helicopters.* Mankato, MN: Capstone Press, Incorporated, 1996.

RESOURCES

AH-64 Apache
www.boeing.com/rotorcraft/military/ah64d/ah64d.htm
This site provides a detailed history of the AH-64 Apache helicopter.

Aviation Through the Ages
http://tqjunior.advanced.org/3785/
This site details the history of flying and famous aviators, with a gallery of images.

Boeing
www.boeing.com
This is the official site of the Boeing company, makers of the Apache Longbow.

The Rotorhead
www.rotorhead.org
This site contains information about many types of helicopters. Check out pictures of the AH-64!

INDEX

INDEX

About the Author

Matthew Pitt is a freelance writer living in Brooklyn, New York. He has written several magazine articles and short stories while living in cities such as Austin, Texas, Washington, D.C., and Los Angeles, California.